W9-BIP-987

DISCARDED

Pokémon ADVENTURES

Volume 9
Perfect Square Edition

Story by **HIDENORI KUSAKA**
Art by **MATO**

© 2010 The Pokémon Company International.
© 1995-2010 Nintendo/Creatures Inc./GAME FREAK inc.
TM, ®, and character names are trademarks of Nintendo.
POCKET MONSTERS SPECIAL Vol. 9
by Hidenori KUSAKA, MATO
© 1997 Hidenori KUSAKA, MATO
All rights reserved.
Original Japanese edition published by SHOGAKUKAN.
English translation rights in the United States of America, Canada, the
United Kingdom, Ireland, Australia and New Zealand arranged with SHOGAKUKAN.

English Adaptation/Gerard Jones
Translation/Kaori Inoue
Touch-up & Lettering/Annaliese Christman
Design/Sam Elzway
Editor/Jann Jones

The stories, characters and incidents mentioned
in this publication are entirely fictional.

No portion of this book may be reproduced or transmitted in any form or
by any means without written permission from the copyright holders.

Printed in the U.S.A.

Published by VIZ Media, LLC
P.O. Box 77010
San Francisco, CA 94107

10 9
First printing, October 2010
Ninth printing, December 2016

3133304690799 2

PARENTAL ADVISORY
POKÉMON ADVENTURES
is rated A and is suitable
for readers of all ages.
ratings.viz.com

PERFECT SQUARE

ⅵƵ media

www.perfectsquare.com

www.viz.com

POKÉMON™ ADVENTURES

GOLD & SILVER

9 VOLUME NINE

Story by
Hidenori Kusaka
Art by Mato

CHARACTERS THUS FAR...

POKÉMON

Aibo (Aipom)

Gold, a kid from New Bark Town in the region of Johto, is hot on the trail of Silver, a thief who stole a Totodile from Professor Elm and a Pokédex from Professor Oak...

Joined by Exbo, a Cyndaquil from Elm's lab and a friend of the kidnapped Totodile, Gold catches Silver.

Exbo (Cyndaquil)

▲ Gold

He can be reckless and relies too much on luck. But his sense of justice when it comes to Pokémon is second to none... and his battle skills get better every day!

MAIN JOURNEY

▲ Silver

A young man of few words. Though there seems to be a reason behind his actions, his mission is a mysterious one. He is a more skilled Trainer than Gold.

Sneasel

Joey ▼

◀ Professor Oak

Gold and Silver finally battle, but then they join against a common foe—Team Rocket, who everyone thinks was destroyed years ago! Once again, Silver slips away. Now Gold really wants to know what he's up to!

Sunbo (Sunkern)

Polibo (Poliwag)

Professor Elm ▶

CONTENTS

SILVER

15

16

20

HUH?
OH.
YEAH,
RIGHT.
CARE-
FUL.

GOLD!!
ARE
YOU
LISTEN-
ING?!

THAT
GUY'S
GOT
NERVE
SAYING
SILVER'S
BETTER
THAN...

THE KID
WITH THE
CROCONAW
HE WAS
TALKING
ABOUT...

...HAS
GOT TO BE
SILVER. THE
TOTODILE
MUST HAVE
EVOLVED.

THE KID
CAME INTO
CONTACT
WITH THE
MASKED
MAN.

SILVER,
NEW
DATA.

PIRIRI

I'M
ON
IT.

I WANT
YOU TO
KEEP UP
WITH
YOUR
SURVEIL-
LANCE
OF THE
MASKED
MAN.

IT
WAS
IN THE
FOREST
IN QUES-
TION.
AFTERWARD
LIGHT WAS
SEEN
EMANATING
FROM THE
SHRINE... BUT
THE MASKED
MAN FAILED
TO OBTAIN
THE LIGHT.

22

24

...THE ZEPHYR BADGE.

ONE OF THE SACRED RESPONSIBILITIES OF THE GYM LEADER IS TO GUARD THIS...

FSH

FALKNER.

YOU ARE TO BESTOW THIS BADGE ONLY ON THOSE WHOM YOU DEEM TRULY WORTHY.

TRAINERS WILL SOON BE COMING FROM ALL OVER TO CHALLENGE YOU IN YOUR GYM... YOU MUST TEST THEIR ABILITIES.

I PASSED... USING THE SKARMORY WE CAPTURED TOGETHER.

HOO

YOU WANTED HEAT?!!

WELL, GOLD...

BLAH BLAH

FUR-THER-MORE...

I WISH I KNEW HOW TO FIND YOU NOW... OR KNEW HOW YOU'RE DOING, AT LEAST...

...HUGE!!

THAT CITY... IS REALLY...

GOLDENROD CITY

AND ALL THOSE LIGHTS! UP HERE IT'S MIDNIGHT... AND DOWN THERE IT'S AS BRIGHT AS NOON!

OH WELL. GUESS WE CAN WORRY ABOUT THAT TOMORROW. G'NIGHT, GANG.

YAWW

TOO BAD I'VE GOT NO MONEY.

SHK SHK

IT'S SUPPOSED TO BE FULL OF STORES AND GAME CORNERS AND EVERYTHING!

PiPi

28

30

33

34

36

HAS THAT LINE EVER ACTUALLY WORKED FOR YOU?!

WAIT!!!

106
How Do You Do, Sudowoodo?

WHITNEY IS DISPLAYING ALL HER EXPERIENCE, JUMPING OUT TO AN EARLY LEAD!

MOBILE STUDIO 1

THE POKÉMON BATTLE RACE IS UNDER WAY!!

THE KID'S GOOD ON A SKATEBOARD!

BUT GOLD IS CLOSING IN!

FSSH

—RUNNING RIGHT ALONGSIDE HER!

AND SHE'S GOT TWO POKÉMON— SMEARGLE AND MILTANK—

40

42

HOW AM I SUPPOSED TO WIN WITH THAT THING IN THE WAY?!

LIKE YOU SAID...

W-W-WHAT KIND OF TREE IS THIS?!

THAT'S MY LINE!!

FWOOSH

BRR SPPU BRR

WAK WAK

TIME TO GO ALL OUT! AIBO! SUNBO! POLIBO!

ARE THOSE... FOOTSTEPS?!!

!!

TMM TMM TMM

NOW WHAT?!

WEIRD.

THE ONLY THING IT REACTED TO WAS POLIBO'S WATER ATTACK...

43

EEEYAAA!!!

FIRST AN INDESTRUCTIBLE TREE BLOCKING THE ROUTE ...

NOW A WILD POKÉMON!!

VIP VIP

TOOM

IT'LL CRUSH YOU WITHOUT BATTING AN EYE!!

WE HAVE TO STRIKE FIRST!!

VSH

DON'T JUST STAND THERE, IDIOT!! THAT'S RHYDON!!

IS IT LOOKING FOR SOMETHING?

45

46

WAIT A MINUTE... YOU MEAN...

YOU'RE A POKÉMON?!!

NOD

!

VOOP VOOP

VOOP VOOP

THAT CRAZY RHYDON— ARE YOU WHAT IT WAS AFTER?!

NOD

No. 185
Sudowoodo
Imitation Pokémon
Height 3' 11''
Weight 83.8 lbs
Disguises as tree to avoid being attacked. Dislikes water, includin' rain.
Cry Area F

MAN, THAT WAS THE BEST TREE IMITATION I'VE EVER SEEN!

YOU HIDING FROM SOMETH... OH!!

BUT WHAT'S THE BIG IDEA?!

47

48

50

STUDIO

THE RACE MAY BE CANCELED, BUT THE WINNER'S CLEAR!

NEH HEH HEH HEH HEH!!

||You got lucky!||

AND WHO HAD TO RESCUE HIS OPPONENT?! WAHAHA!

I MEAN, WHO MOVED THE IMMOVABLE TREE, HUH?

SPCH

HEY!

HONK

I GUESS I DESERVE A LITTLE RESPECT, EH, SMEARGLE?

NEXT TIME, PUNK... WE'RE GONNA HAVE A **REAL** MATCH!!

UM, GOLD? HOW MANY AUTOGRAPHS DID YOU SAY?

WHY, YOU CHEESY LITTLE—

WAM WOO

ALL THOSE MOVES—WERE FROM THAT THING?!

YOU DISGUISED A POKÉ BALL AS A POOL BALL?!

Heh heh. Clever, huh?

FOMP

PLI

FyOOOOOO

GAME

GET OUTTA HERE!!

She totally dug me.

A CALL ON MY POKÉ-GEAR! MAYBE IT'S THAT PICNICKER GIRL!

PRRRRT

PIP

HMPH.

SOME PEOPLE CAN'T TAKE A JOKE.

YEEPS! PROFESSOR?!

I HEARD YOU ON THE RADIO THE OTHER DAY.

HAVING FUN?!

Professor Elm

!!

WELL, GOLD.

Exbo
Polibo
Sunbo
Aibo
Sudo
Egg

WHAT'S THE STATUS OF YOUR POKÉMON TEAM AT PRESENT?

EXBO... THAT'S YOUR CYNDAQUIL... IS DOING GREAT!

SO ARE AIBO THE AIPOM, POLIBO THE POLIWAG...

...SUNBO THE SUNKERN... AND A NEW ONE...

...SUDOBO THE SUDOWOODO.

OH, AND THE EGG!!

IT'S... WELL... STILL AN EGG!

CLICK. BEEP BEEP BEEP.

GEEZ. BOSSY, BOSSY!

PROMISE ME YOU'LL KEEP A VERY CLOSE EYE ON IT!

GOOD. THE EGG IS WHY I'M CALLING. EVEN I DON'T KNOW WHAT KINDS OF CHANGES IT MAY GO THROUGH.

58

61

THUK

SIZZLE

GNAAA

66

70

72

74

WE WERE TAKING CARE OF TWO POKÉMON... DON'T EVEN KNOW WHAT THEY WERE.

WHAT ?!!

SUDDENLY THEY WERE GONE... AND THERE WAS AN EGG!

GEEZ... SO NOTHING TO REPORT TO ELM... AGAIN.

WE KEEP WATCHING TO SEE IF ANYONE ELSE LAYS ONE, BUT NO LUCK.

NO BETTER PLACE FOR TIPS ON RAISING THEM RIGHT!

YOU'RE AT THE FAMOUS POKÉMON DAY CARE!

WAIT !!!

CIAO!

WELL, GUESS I'LL BE GOING!

REALLY ?!

YOU COULD MAKE THOSE POKÉMON OF YOURS MIGHTY STRONG!

81

83

84

THESE POKÉMON ARE ALL VETERAN FIGHTERS!

WOM

YEEE!

WAP

ACK!

FOSH

EXBO! SMOKE-SCREEN!!

WELL, I'LL SHOW 'EM!!

EEP

TIKTIKTIKTIK

TOGEBO! METRO-NOME!!

I KNOW, I KNOW!

THAT'S NOT EXACTLY WHAT I'D CALL AN IMPENETRABLE DEFENSE.

88

HOOSH

COULD BE WORSE. BOY'S GOT POTENTIAL.

HOW IS IT GOING SWEETIE?

I GUESS THAT'S WHAT OAK SAW IN HIM WHEN HE GAVE HIM THE POKÉDEX.

...WHILE WE OLD FOLKS HARDLY HAVE TO LIFT A FINGER. I'D CALL THAT A NEAT TRICK!

...AND LETTING OURS BLOW OFF SOME STEAM...

HE'S GIVING HIS POKÉMON SOME USEFUL PRACTICE...

SURE I DO! BUT I JUST DON'T KNOW IF...

THIS IS WHAT THEY'VE GOT TO GO THROUGH IF THEY'RE GONNA GET STRONGER! YOU **DO** WANT 'EM TO GET STRONGER?

YOU'RE NOT GIVING UP ALREADY?

NO WAY! BUT...ISN'T THIS KINDA ROUGH ON MY POKÉMON...?

HEY, GRANDMA!

BRRR BRRR

EXBO, WHAT'S WRONG?!

PING

90

94

96

NH...

WHO... ARE YOU...?

RRRM!

SHMP

WE GOTTA GET TO THE TOP! WHERE THE LIGHT WAS!

YO!! ANY-BODY HERE?!!

TM TM TM

WELL THEN, WE BETTER BE QUICK!!

FINE. THEN YOU TAKE HER.

HEY!

YOU EXPECT ME TO BELIEVE YOU'D HELP ANOTHER ...

WHA ...?

?

WHAT'S HE UP TO...?

A SCULPTURE OF A POKÉMON?!

HO-OH

"HO-OH," HUH...?

101

105

106

POLIBO EVOLVED AGAIN?!

BUT... IT'S NOT POLIWRATH?!

BBOOSH

WHIRL-POOL!!

FOR WATER POWER, POLITOED IS BEST.

WHAT?!

IT'S A TRADE EVOLUTION.

THIS POKÉMON HAS **TWO** FINAL FORMS.

WHAT DID YOU JUST DO?!

WD

OWW!

TM

108

110

114

AND IT'S GOING TO KEEP CRUSHING THE GROUND— UNTIL YOU'VE GOT NOWHERE TO STAND! THEN WE'LL SEE HOW LONG YOUR POKÉMON CAN CARRY YOU!

TAKE DOWN!! ROCK SMASH!! IT HAS THE POWER TO SHATTER THE EARTH UNDER A WHOLE CITY!!

...WHEN THE GROUND GETS SHAKEN BADLY ENOUGH?

BUT YOU KNOW WHAT HAPPENS, DON'T YOU...

THINK SO?

...

IT'S CALLED... LIQUE-FACTION!

119

120

127

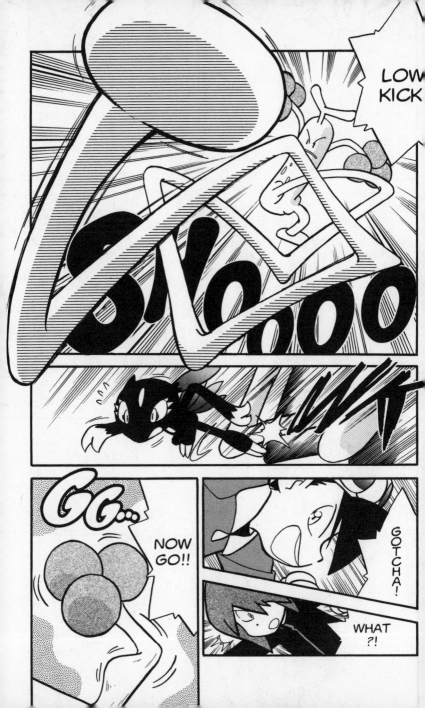

140

VNNN

WSH

...

...FOR YOUR EFFORTS, I'LL ANSWER YOUR QUESTION.

YOU MEAN ...?

IT'S SAID THAT THE TIN TOWER IS WHERE THE LEGENDARY POKÉMON HO-OH NESTS.

"CALL FORTH"?!

PAP

TEAM ROCKET ATTACKED ECRUTEAK IN ORDER TO CALL FORTH HO-OH.

TEAM ROCKET HOPES THAT DESTROYING THE TIN TOWER WILL TRIGGER HO-OH'S HOMING INSTINCTS.

YOU MEAN THEY DESTROYED THE CITY... JUST TO BRING SOME POKÉMON BACK TO ITS NEST?!

AS FOR MY MISSION... IT'S TO CRUSH THEM.

NOT EVEN IF I HAVE TO BREAK THE LAW.

...I CAN'T BE CHOOSY ABOUT THE MEANS.

IN ORDER TO ACHIEVE THOSE ENDS...

AND ALSO TO FOLLOW HO-OH.

142

145

FHOOOOO

THE BIG FLYING-TYPE POKÉMON THAT DISAPPEARED A YEAR AGO IN JOHTO.

I LOOKED INTO WHAT YOU ASKED ME ABOUT BEFORE...

I NEED A SKILLED TRAINER.

THE THING'S DANGEROUS. I CAN'T HANDLE IT MYSELF.

...

BUT... WHO ELSE CAN I TURN TO?

HM

THE ONLY REASON I WAS ABLE TO WIN A YEAR AGO WAS BECAUSE OF EVERYONE ELSE'S HELP!

IN THAT CASE, I'M HARDLY THE ONE TO ASK!

VOOP

HOW MANY REDS DO YOU KNOW?

THAT RED?

HOW ABOUT RED?

148

ZWOOSH

112

Raise the Red Gyarados

EEYOW!!

A MASS OUTBREAK OF GYARADOS!!

WHAT'S GOIN' ON?

YOU! KID! RUN! NOW!

YAAAA

MAN... THAT'S ONE ACTIVE LAKE...!

IF THEY ALL START RAMPAGING, THEY COULD DESTROY THE TOWN!!

156

158

THE TRANSMITTER IS...THIS POKÉMON?!

GOLD, WAIT!!

I HATE TO HURT A POKÉMON... BUT WHAT CAN I DO?!

GOOD THINK- ING!!

THAT'S A WILD POKÉ- MON! CAPTURE IT...

...AND IT'LL NO LONGER FUNCTION THE SAME!

162

166

168

BUT ITS CRYSTALLINE STRUCTURE MATCHED THAT...

...ONLY BY THE GYM LEADERS!

...OF THE TRAINER BADGES HELD...

I ALMOST CAN'T BRING MYSELF TO BELIEVE IT...

I'VE COMPLETED MY ANALYSIS OF THAT GOLD POWDER.

IT'S HARD TO IMAGINE A MORE DANGEROUS OPPONENT THAN A GYM LEADER!

THE MASKED MAN YOU FOUGHT IN ILEX FOREST MAY BE A FORMER GYM LEADER! BUT WE DON'T KNOW WHICH ONE!

NO MATTER WHAT... DON'T FIGHT HIM!

BUT KNOWING YOU, YOU'LL RUSH RIGHT INTO COMBAT WITH HIM!

HMF

THANKS FOR THE WARNING, PROFESSOR...

...

DO YOU UNDERSTAND, GOLD?

174

176

YOU...

I CAUGHT THE ONE YOU WERE USING AS A TRANSMITTER.

THAT MEANS THEY'VE ALL BEEN FREED FROM YOUR CONTROL...

AND THEY'RE ANGRY!! HYPER BEAM!!

FSH

191

THERE'S NO WAY.

LOOK, GUYS. I APPRECIATE YOUR CONCERN, BUT...

SHE'S RIGHT, RED. YOU SHOULD BE RESTING.

BUT IN THAT CONDITION... TOMORROW...

BECAUSE TOMORROW'S EXAM DAY... FOR THE VIRIDIAN GYM LEADER.

115 Forretress of Solitude

...

...

NOW... LET'S KEEP TRAINING!!

194

195

ANOTHER FORRETRESS— AND IT'S UNLEASHED SPIKES!!

SHM

!!

SHM

SNOR! BELLY DRUM!!

NOW RETURN!

BOM

FUAAA

SAUR— SWEET SCENT!

SNORLAX IS NO BETTER AGAINST SPIKES THAN VENUSAUR!

WHAT'S HE PLAN— NING?

BIDDYBOM

BLOOB BLOOB M

WHAT'S HE UP TO?

※ SEE POKÉMON ADVENTURES VOLUME 7

214

215

WATCH OUT FOR POKÉMON ADVENTURES VOLUME 10!

ADVENTURE ROUTE MAP 9

FROM ILEX FOREST TO MAHOGANY AND THE LAKE OF RAGE! (WITH A LOOK AT THE VETERAN TRAINERS' MOVEMENTS TOO!)

Routes in Johto & Kanto!!

LAKE OF RAGE

Chapter 112

Chapter 113

Chapter 114

MAHOGANY TOWN

VS QUILAVA

VS ARIADOS

VIRIDIAN CITY

Chapter 115

Chapter 116

RED TRAINED ON THE OUTSKIRTS OF PALLET TOWN, THE EXAM TOOK PLACE AT VIRIDIAN GYM.

PALLET TOWN

VS SCIZOR

VS FORRETRESS

WOK

FALSE SWIPE

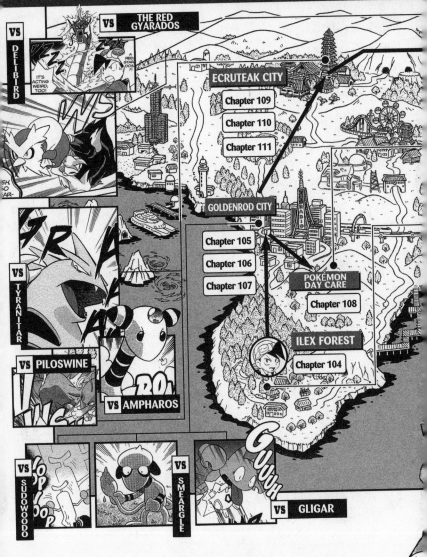

"GOTTA CATCH 'EM ALL!!"
ADVENTURE ROUTE MAP 9

VS DELIBIRD

VS THE RED GYARADOS

IT'S ACTING WEIRD, TOO!

A RED GYARADOS?!

ECRUTEAK CITY

Chapter 109

Chapter 110

Chapter 111

GOLDENROD CITY

Chapter 105

Chapter 106

Chapter 107

POKÉMON DAY CARE

Chapter 108

ILEX FOREST

Chapter 104

VS TYRANITAR

VS PILOSWINE

VS AMPHAROS

VS SUDOWOODO

VS SMEARGLE

VS GLIGAR

GUUUH

POKÉDEX

MAIN CHARACTER: SILVER
BADGES: 4
POKÉDEX : 10 POKÉMON

NUMBER SEEN
54
NUMBER CAUGHT
10

Silver is always seeking Pokémon who'll help him fulfill his objective!

The Team Thus Far:

Seems to favor Dark-types. An attack-oriented team.

TEAM SILVER

SNEASEL: LV 36
TYPE 1 / DARK
TYPE 2 / ICE
TRAINER / SILVER
NO.215

THE TEAM LEADER!
BEATS OPPONENTS
WITH SHARP CLAWS,
SHARP WITS AND
FAST MOVES!

MURKROW: LV 29
TYPE 1 / DARK
TYPE 2 / FLYING
TRAINER / SILVER
NO.198

LOOKS LIKE THE WINGS
OF DARKNESS AS IT
CARRIES SILVER—AND
GIVES HIM A BIG
ADVANTAGE IN NIGHT
BATTLES!

URSARING: LV 35
TYPE 1 / NORMAL
TRAINER / SILVER
NO.217

THE HEAVIEST MEMBER
OF THE TEAM, CAUGHT
USING A HEAVY BALL—
AND A HEAVY-DUTY
FIGHTER!

CROCONAW: LV 29
TYPE 1 / WATER
TRAINER / SILVER
NO.159

Croconaw
evolved from
the Totodile that
Silver stole from
Professor Elm's lab.
Kingdra evolved
during a trade
with Gold. A rare
red Gyarados
appears. Why does
he want three
Water-types? And
who did he borrow
Tyranitar from?
There's a hint in
the Poké Ball
it came out
of…

KINGDRA: LV 33
TYPE 1 / WATER
TYPE 2 / DRAGON
TRAINER / SILVER
NO.230

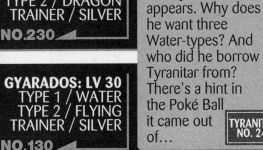

**TYRANITAR
NO. 248**

GYARADOS: LV 30
TYPE 1 / WATER
TYPE 2 / FLYING
TRAINER / SILVER
NO.130

Message from
Hidenori Kusaka

For me the 21st century began when I got my first Game Boy Advance... a Pokémon Center limited edition! I was totally excited! Suicune blue! (Of course, I get excited easily.) I still play it to get in the right creative mood...

Message from
MATO

Gold, Silver, Red, Blue, Yellow and all those Pokémon... The four years I've spent with them have seemed long, but it also feels like just yesterday that we first met. It's an amazing feeling. We've been able to have this great run because of the enthusiasm of you, our fans. And so, with deep gratitude, we bring you this book!

More Adventures Coming Soon...

The journey continues! In order to assist Professor Oak's research, a young Trainer, Crystal, hits the streets with a new Pokédex in hand! Her goal is to capture all kinds of wild Pokémon! And what will happen now that the Legendary Pokémon Suicune has awakened?!

AVAILABLE NOW!

Pokémon

ADVENTURES

HEARTGOLD & SOULSILVER

Story by HIDENORI KUSAKA
Art by SATOSHI YAMAMOTO

In this **two-volume** thriller, troublemaker Gold and feisty Silver must team up again to find their old enemy Lance and the Legendary Pokémon Arceus!

Available now!

© 2013 Pokémon.
© 1995-2013 Nintendo/Creatures Inc./GAME FREAK inc.
TM and ® and character names are trademarks of Nintendo.
POCKET MONSTERS SPECIAL © 1997 Hidenori KUSAKA, Satoshi YAMAMOTO/SHOGAKUKAN

A NEW MEGA ADVENTURE!

THE SERIES
XY

Ash Ketchum's journey continues in
Pokémon the Series: XY
as he arrives in the Kalos region,
a land bursting with beauty, full of
new Pokémon to be discovered!

24
ACTION-PACKED
EPISODES!

Pick up **Pokémon the Series: XY** today!
IN STORES NATIONWIDE
visit **viz.com** for more information

TV Y7 FV

DVD VIDEO

©2015 Pokémon.
©1997-2014 Nintendo, Creatures, GAME FREAK, TV Tokyo, ShoPro, JR Kikaku. TM, ® Nintendo.

VIZ MEDIA

The Pokémon Company
INTERNATIONAL

PERFECT SQUARE

viz MEDIA
www.viz.com

RATED
A
ALL AGES
ratings.viz.com

© 2013 Pokémon.
©1995-2013 Nintendo/Creatures Inc./GAME FREAK inc. TM, ®, and character names are trademarks of Nintendo.
POKÉMON BW (Black • White) BAKUSHO 4KOMA MANGA ZENSHU © 2011 Santa HARUKAZE/SHOGAKUKAN

Pokémon™

BLACK AND WHITE

MEET POKÉMON TRAINERS
BLACK AND WHITE

Meet Pokémon Trainer Black! His entire life, Black has dreamed of winning the Pokémon League... Now Black embarks on a journey to explore the Unova region and fill a Pokédex for Professor Juniper. Time for Black's first Pokémon Trainer Battle ever!

Who will Black choose as his next Pokémon? Who would *you* choose?

Plus, meet Pokémon Snivy, Tepig, Oshawott and many more new Pokémon of the unexplored Unova region!

Story by
HIDENORI KUSAKA

Art by
SATOSHI YAMAMOTO

$4.99 USA | $6.99 CAN

Inspired by the hit video games
Pokémon Black Version and *Pokémon White Version!*

Available Now
at your local bookstore or comic store

© 2011 Pokémon.
©1995-2011 Nintendo/Creatures Inc./GAME FREAK inc.
Pokémon properties are trademarks of Nintendo.
POCKET MONSTER SPECIAL © 1997 Hidenori KUSAKA,
Satoshi YAMAMOTO/Shogakukan

THIS IS THE END OF THIS GRAPHIC NOVEL!

To properly enjoy this VIZ Media graphic novel, please turn it around and begin reading from right to left.

This book has been printed in the original Japanese format in order to preserve the orientation of the original artwork. Have fun with it!

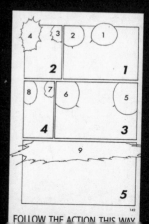

FOLLOW THE ACTION THIS WAY